MÜLLER'S ORPHANAG

Any visitor to the Ashley Down area of Bristol cannot go
prominent buildings of the former Müller Orphanages. When th
stood in a sparsely populated area; now they are in the
development. From certain vantage points they still rise up to don
large, solid, imposing, stone-built walls. Today they are used by .... College of Arts
and Technology but for over 100 years they were home to a large number of destitute and
orphaned children. Over 18,000 children were cared for in the Homes from the 1840's
onwards.

The work had small beginnings when in Wilson Street, St. Paul's, the first orphan was
taken from the streets in 1836, and grew to over 2,000 orphans being cared for at a time.
The buildings and the work are a testimony to a God who answered a man's prayer
faithfully for many years and also a testimony to that man, George Müller, who, having
become a Christian in 1825 after a very dissolute early life, and who lived a long life of
devoted prayer and faith, wanted to demonstrate the faithfulness, dependability and
reality of God. George Müller never asked anyone for money during the entirety of his
Christian life; only God in prayer and he was never disappointed. God spoke to him so
clearly through Psalm 81: 10: *"Open thy mouth wide and I will fill it"*. God did that
abundantly. In 1841 Müller wrote "Morning by morning God is inspecting our stores.
After breakfast there were no means for dinner, and then the Lord provided the dinner
for more than one hundred persons. After dinner there were no means for tea, and yet
the Lord provided the tea; and all this without one single human being having been
informed about our need."

No-one had ever sought to build such a work based totally on prayer but he built and
ran the Homes, fed, clothed, cared for, educated and gave a fresh start in life to
thousands of needy children. Above all, the children benefited from a level of Christian
care which was amongst the earliest examples of the nineteenth century Christian social
revolution which raised up Shaftesbury, Barnardo and others. Many children you see in
the pages of this book may have died of neglect had he not stepped out in faith. Over the
years of his long life (1805-1898) George Müller received one and a half million pounds in
direct answer to believing prayer without even asking for funds and he is known world-
wide as a man of remarkable vision and faith.

The work that he founded amongst children and families still continues today and
although the ways in which care is given are now different, the principles he lived by and
on which he established the work are still the same today. Many children and families
are still benefiting from the same Christian love and care; some are cared for in their old
age in a Müller Home too!

May I encourage you to read and enjoy the photographs in this book and perhaps you
will be challenged by this work of faith. In a world where there is often so little hope and
love and care, there is hope and love and care because the God who provided for George
Müller and the work you will see on the following pages is the same God today.

If you would like to know more about George Müller, his work and his faith, please
write to, or telephone, the headquarters of the work:-

The Executive Director
The George Müller Foundation
Müller House
7 Cotham Park
Bristol BS6 6DA
Telephone: 0117 924 5001
Fax: 0117 924 4855

Books concerning the work are available and there is also a small museum which can
be visited during office hours.

Julian Marsh
Executive Director
The George Müller Foundation

MÜLLER'S ORPHANAGE

1. George Müller, founder of the Ashley Down Orphan Homes, was born in Kroppenstaedt, Prussia on 27 September 1805. He opened his first Orphanage in Bristol, at No.6 Wilson Street, St. Pauls in a rented house in April 1836. In October of that year he rented No.1 and in November 1837 rented No.3, then in the autumn of 1843 he opened No.4 Wilson Street.

MR. MÜLLER'S STUDY.

2. George Müller's study where a lot of his work was co-ordinated at Ashley Down, together with his world wide work with the Scriptural Knowledge Institution which he founded in 1834. The desk can still be seen at the present Müller House in Cotham Park.

THE
BRISTOL MIRACLE

*An account of God's faithfulness
to the work of*

GEORGE MÜLLER

GEORGE MÜLLER THE MAN

George Müller was an ordinary man, but his undeniable faith, implicit trust and love for God has the same impact on the world today as when he died in 1898. This continues to be an inspiration and witness to all who commit their lives to God.

One of the many fascinating aspects of George Müller's life is that it illustrates very simply the power of God. There are those who find it difficult to accept the authenticity of much of the scriptures and view many of the remarkable stories with scepticism. George Müller received £1,500,000 in answer to prayer without ever needing to ask for funds. At present day prices, this would be well over £75,000,000. Had this happened two or three thousand years ago the same sceptics would, undoubtedly, have questioned its authenticity. As it happened in the latter part of the nineteenth century with modern records and factual evidence, the facts can be challenged but certainly not disputed.

What is perhaps even more remarkable is that it is the SAME TODAY. The George Müller Foundation makes no appeals, yet through the same trust in God, money is received almost daily for the Homes, for the Elderly work and also for The Scriptural Knowledge Institution, which aids the work of missionaries world-wide.

George Müller was the faithful servant whom God used. This fact has an intriguing parallel with many Biblical characters.

GOD CHOOSES ALL TYPES

God often chose ordinary men, sometimes men with an inglorious and doubtful past, men who often mocked the faith and men with whom a great deal of patience was needed because of their reluctance to turn away from the 'good life'. George Müller had been all of these types.

George Müller was born in Kroppenstaedt, a Prussian village, on the 27th September 1805. The son of a Tax Collector, he did not become a Christian until he was twenty years of age. His father wanted him to enter the ministry but only so that he could retire to the ease of his son's manse. Despite kindness and generosity continually shown by his father, George Müller was an habitual thief, inveterate liar and indeed he later said there was almost no sin into which he had not fallen. He even had the audacity to become a confirmed member of the Lutheran Church and take Communion in spite of being well aware of his sinful ways.

George Müller's conversion was dramatic! Many of his sinful ways he

1

relinquished at once and as understanding of the Christian way of life increased so he dedicated his life to Jesus Christ. When he came to England in 1829 he formed a friendship with a quiet, godly and scholarly Scotsman named Henry Craik. This became a life-long friendship and under God's guidance they formed a great spiritual partnership in the Gospel and in children's work.

Through the work of the Orphan Homes and the Scriptural Knowledge Institution, both of which Mr Müller founded, many responded to the gospel and heard the call to dedicate their lives to God. The work continues today on the same principles - and the witness to God's faithfulness is still used to the glory of God.

AN INSPIRATION

The most significant aspect of George Müller's 93 years on earth was his absolute obedience to the will of God. It is this example which inspired and continues to inspire men to know and exercise that faith which God requires of us all. The fact that the Spirit of God transformed a rebellious, sinful and self-determined young man to become such a man of God must surely give rise to hope for each one of us.

'*Blessed is the man who trusts in the Lord*'.

George Müller trusted and his trust was never in vain.

THE WASTED YEARS

George Müller was born in 1805 and until his conversion to the Christian faith in 1825, there was, on his own admission, hardly a sin into which he had not fallen.

He had become an habitual thief, liar, gambler and a cheat, devising cunning and devious methods to fulfil his evil desires. Besides his immoral ways it was George Müller's need for alcoholic drink that caused many of his problems. Even when his mother lay dying he was found roaming the streets in a drunken state.

THE PRODIGAL SON

The similarities between George Müller's early life and the parable of the Prodigal Son are quite remarkable, a fact not unnoticed by many writers and commentators.

In 1810 George Müller moved with his family from that Prussian village of Kroppenstaedt to nearby Heimersleben, some four miles away. He and his brother received no real parental control and their father, being very generous, gave them plenty of money. They were encouraged to keep records of their spending, but that is where parental discipline and control ended.

George Müller regularly stole money from his father, invariably when collecting debts on his father's behalf by handing over much less than he had collected. His father often had to make up missing money and on one occasion a successfully laid trap caused George

2

Müller to be punished, but he was unrepentant.

George Müller was sent to a classical school at Halberstaedt hoping to become a Lutheran clergyman. Despite being a brilliant pupil he continued his sinful ways. His stealing became more compulsive and on one occasion he managed to retain all but one twelfth of his confirmation fees which his father had given him for confirmation classes.

DECEIT, LIES AND PRISON

Once George Müller embarked upon a remarkable period of deceit and lies as he went from one hotel to another, often in the company of a woman, living a 'playboy' life, but with no money. After pawning valuable possessions and leaving his remaining belongings at one hotel as security, the law caught up with him and he ended up in prison. Even in prison George Müller told the most unbelievable lies to impress a fellow prisoner.

After a month in prison his father bailed him out, settled his debts and beat him. For a while George Müller tried to please his father and indeed, tried to change his ways. It was not long however, before he was in debt again and this time he concocted a story of having been robbed and was more than compensated by his sympathetic friends. Further, he managed to get some of his debts written off and payment of the remaining ones delayed. When his friends eventually discovered the truth this did not seriously concern him.

The last sinful escapade came when he was at Halle University studying theology. With three fellow students they forged papers and documents so that they could go on a vacation of worldly pleasure in Switzerland. George Müller even then managed to cheat his friends by having charge of the money and, through devious means, only paid two thirds of that paid by the others.

After the Swiss holiday one member of the party, Beta, who was an old friend and fellow student of George Müller told him of a prayer meeting which he often attended. George Müller expressed a desire to go with him and it was that meeting which was to change his whole life.

'For God so loved the world, that He gave His one and only Son, that whoever believes in Him shall not perish but have eternal life.'

It pleased God to teach George Müller something of that precious truth.

THE TURNING POINT

George Müller's conversion in November 1825 was dramatic and his whole direction, purpose and way of life changed immediately.

He was introduced to the prayer meeting by his friend Beta and upon arrival was greeted with *'Come as often as you please; house and heart are open to you.'* This welcome touched George Müller very much. The singing of hymns, study of the Bible and reading of a printed sermon made a deep impression and he felt this night he would find 'something' for which he had been searching all his life. The genuine love, great joy and deep humility in the hearts of the members of that group had a profound effect on George Müller but perhaps the turning point was when they all knelt to pray. He had never seen this before, let alone knelt to pray himself, and the whole meeting breathed such a spiritual atmosphere that he entered upon an entirely new experience! He was born again! No longer an idle and lazy character, but a disciple of the Living God.

Some time later George Müller said about that evening, *'I understood something of the reason why the Lord Jesus died on the cross and suffered agonies in the Garden of Gethsemane; even that thus, bearing the punishment due to us, we might not have to bear it ourselves. And therefore, apprehending in some measure the love of Jesus for my soul, I was constrained to love Him in return.'*

George Müller continued his theological studies at Halle University and within two months of his conversion to the Christian faith decided to become a missionary. This decision angered his father so much that he withdrew his son's financial support which left George Müller dependent on God alone.

A TEST OF FAITH

Without his father's allowance George Müller was penniless. Very shortly after committing the problem to God he was asked to teach German to visiting American professors and for this he was paid much more than he actually needed.

The greatest obstacle George Müller had to overcome was the acquisition of a passport to attend a missionary training school in London, because he was expected to serve his national service. After much prayer he went through with the signing up process for the Army and following a series of medicals he was discharged from active service for life as being medically unfit.

George Müller in 1829 made his way to London to train as a missionary to the Jews. After only a short time at the missionary training school he became seriously ill and nearly died. It was whilst recuperating in the Devon town of Teignmouth that George Müller's life was to take another change of direction.

PREACHING

George Müller met up with Henry Craik, a Scotsman who was to become his closest friend and it was this quiet, godly and learned man who taught George Müller the need to wholly trust in, and be obedient to, the will of God. After resigning from the Mission school to take up preaching engagements, George Müller eventually accepted the Pastorate of a Church in Teignmouth with an honorarium of £50 per annum. He felt that God would provide all his needs and that he should be wholly dependent upon Him. From that moment on, until his death in 1898,

George Müller grew in obedience and trust in God for everything.

THE CHANGE OF DIRECTION

With the help of his very good friend Henry Craik, he gained a much greater understanding of the Scriptures and the will of God. During this period of learning in Teignmouth, George Müller realised that many preachers failed to communicate the truths of the Gospel message and tended to read printed sermons which were often apologetic, lacked conviction and inspiration. As George Müller began to preach God's Word in a straight, dynamic and forthright manner, he was continually encouraged by the response of many listeners and the increasing number of conversions. Despite the growing response to his preaching there were many who reacted strongly against his direct approach, but somehow they seemed powerless to do anything about it, except listen.

THE MOVE TO BRISTOL

In 1830 George Müller married Mary Groves who became a true companion and support for the changing years which lay ahead. After two years he knew that his time in Teignmouth was coming to an end and although he was settled and very happy, he sensed that a move was imminent.

Henry Craik had already moved to Bristol and when he wrote to his best friend inviting him to make the same move, George Müller knew this call was from God. So in 1832 George and Mary Müller left the Devon town of Teignmouth for Bristol where God had a plan prepared for His now faithful servant.

THE FOUNDATION OF THE SCRIPTURAL KNOWLEDGE INSTITUTION

The Scriptural Knowledge Institution, or SKI, as it is known was founded on March 5th, 1834. George Müller laid down four main objectives, which are shown here. In addition, he felt that since this was of God, there would be no patronage, appeals or requests for subscription and that the Institution should never contract any debts. He was convinced that God would provide all resources and meet every need.

Within the first seven months £167 had been received and by May 1894 the figure had risen to half a million pounds. The institution still flourishes today with the same principles, although there are some changes to meet today's needs. Just over one hundred years later, in 1997, over three hundred thousand pounds was sent to missionaries working both at home and overseas for their support. Most of that money resulted from donations being channelled through SKI by individuals, Trusts, and churches.

5

The objects of SKI are expressed as follows:-

1   To assist Day-schools, Sunday-schools and Adult-schools, in which instruction is given upon Scriptural principles, and, as far as the Lord may graciously give the means and supply us with suitable teachers, to establish Schools of this kind.

2   To put the children of poor persons to such Day-schools, in order that they may be truly instructed in the ways of God, besides learning those things which are necessary for this life.

3   To circulate the Holy Scriptures.

4   To aid in supplying the wants of Missionaries and Missionary Schools.

Note   *These objectives are as printed in a document entitled 'First Report of the Operations of the Scriptural Knowledge Society for Home and Abroad' and was signed by both George Müller and Henry Craik on the 7th October, 1834.*

The Bethesda Chapel was the next pastoral ministry for George Müller. The large Chapel was run down and the congregation of six looked extremely small, but with a year's guarantee of rent George Müller committed the future needs of the church to God. The membership grew, financial support came and the Bethesda Chapel prospered both materially and spiritually.

Mary Müller had now given birth to daughter Lydia and it was at the time when Bristol was stricken with cholera. The effects of the cholera resulted in a death rate of high proportions, especially among the adults, and countless children became orphaned.

George Müller, as always, committed the whole problem to God and sought guidance as to what should be done.

PRAYER ANSWERED

He also prayed daily for individual conversions and prayed as long as fifty years for some people which illustrates his faith and trust in God. His own father was daily in his prayers and when the opportunity came to visit Heimersleben, George Müller was overjoyed. The re-union with father and brother was a happy one and George Müller's obvious love for God had a profound effect on his father. At the conclusion of the visit Herr Müller said to his son, *'May God help me to follow your example, and to act according to what you have said to me.'*

In 1834 George Müller founded the Scriptural Knowledge Society (later to become Institution - see inset). However, the worsening cholera epidemic and the ever increasing number of homeless children caused him to realise immediate action was required and in 1835 he called a public meeting with a view to opening an Orphan Home. This was a complete step in faith and four days before the meeting, God confirmed that step through the Scripture - *'Open wide your mouth and I will fill it'* (Psalm 81 verse 10).

ORPHAN HOMES OPENED

George Müller asked God for £1,000 and the right people to run such a home. Within five months this had been provided. Mrs Müller, together with friends, began to furnish their own home in Wilson Street in the St Paul's area of Bristol, which was to accommodate thirty girls. The Orphan Homes became the fifth object of SKI. A further three houses in Wilson Street were furnished, catering for a total of 130 children. When in 1845 this number had risen even further without additional premises, George Müller felt the need to erect a purpose built home to accommodate 300 children. This project required a massive sum of £10,000.

Once more George Müller's prayers were answered as the additional money was provided and he bought a rural site at Ashley Down, just outside the city's boundary, well below the advertised asking price. In 1849 the first Home was opened accommodating 300 children. By 1870 there was a total of five Houses at Ashley Down costing over £100,000 and housing more than 2,000 children. All the money and workers came as a direct result of prayer with no debts being incurred and no appeals or requests were ever made. There are many remarkable stories of the answers to prayer and the buildings and the work continue to be a testimony to His faithfulness and grace of God.

'Open wide your mouth and I will fill it.'

George Müller's total obedience was rewarded by the fulfilment of God's promise.

LIFE IN THE ORPHAN HOMES

When George Müller started the Children's Homes his primary objective was not the welfare of the children. His main concern was that it should be seen that God was providing all the needs as a result of prayer and faith, without anyone being asked or approached.

From the time George Müller started the first home in Wilson Street in 1836 with its 30 girls until the completion of the fifth Home at Ashley Down, bringing his total family to more than 2,000 he was faced with all manner of social problems. Disease was the greatest hazard, ranging from outbreaks of cholera to smallpox epidemics. Poor sanitary conditions, open sewers, unclean drinking water, rubbish piled in the street, no provision for removing the dead and no preventative measures against disease, caused a death rate of high proportions. Despite all this and a slow acting Government, George Müller managed through prayer and faith, to protect his 'large family' against such filth and degradation. Indeed the Müller orphans were more fortunate than most.

Although there were some children who did not enjoy life in the Homes, for many of them it became the means of their salvation. The alternative was little food, often no home and the meaning of life became a matter of survival. The future held little or no hope. George Müller provided, through God, hope, love and a family life with a sound Christian foundation.

All the children in the Homes were smartly dressed. The boys were given three suits and those nine years and above wore a smart navy-blue Eton Jacket, waistcoat and corduroy trousers together with a glazed peaked cap. The younger boys wore a blue shirt instead of the jacket and short cloaks were provided for bad weather conditions. The girls wore a navy blue cotton dress which was protected by a cloak, shawl or tippet according to the weather. All girls wore a straw coloured bonnet tied with an attractive band. The girls also had varying hairstyles according to age. For example, the older girls who were capable of doing their own hair were allowed to grow it to shoulder length or longer.

ABOVE THEIR STATION

The education policy which George Müller devised, was of a high standard and comprised a wide variety of subjects. He was often criticised for his high standard of education which was often described as 'above their station'. Only a few years earlier, Dr Andrew Bell had written in his book - 'An experiment in Education' - *There was a risk of elevating by an indiscriminate education, the minds of those doomed to the drudgery of daily labour, above their condition and thereby rendering them discontented and unhappy with their lot.'*

George Müller did not agree. In fact he employed a School Inspector to maintain the high standards. In 1885 the average percentage of all children in their annual examination based on six subjects was 91.1%. Because of the duration of the education provided by George Müller, he was accused of robbing factories, mills and mines of labour. He was not deterred however, and kept the boys until they were 14 and the girls until they were 17.

The children had other duties to perform. Boys learnt to knit and darn socks, make beds, clean shoes, scrub rooms, work in the garden and run errands. The girls helped in the kitchens, sculleries, wash houses and laundries.

Discipline at the Homes was strict but not harsh. Children who exerted an

8

unacceptable influence on others, were expelled. The usual form of punishment was corporal which was an acceptable form of discipline in those days.

There was not a great deal of variation in the food but it was wholesome and regular. Porridge every morning for breakfast and meat for dinner on Mondays, Thursdays and Fridays. On Tuesdays and Sundays a dish of rice and raisins was commonplace. On Saturdays they were served broth with meat in it. Meat was either mutton - known to the children as 'Og' or corned beef. The bread was known as 'Toke' because of the grace said at meals *'We thank thee, Lord, for these tokens of thy love!'* Fresh fruit and eggs were in plentiful supply and milk and water was the usual drink.

Charles Dickens once visited the Orphanage upon hearing rumours of starvation. After inspection, he left wholly satisfied that the children were adequately fed. On special occasions such as George Müller's birthday they were each given cake and an enormous apple dumpling to mark the anniversary. Christmas was also an occasion for special food and one year 150 pheasants were received from a donor in Cornwall.

The annual outing to Purdown, a field within walking distance from the Orphanage, was a most popular event as was Christmas with its trees, decorations, presents, carols, games and parties.

The children were awakened at six in the morning and after breakfast at eight there was a Bible reading and a time of prayer.

The evening session often included an outside guest speaker.

No child left the Müller Homes until employment had been found for them. The boys were apprenticed to a trade and some with the ability to teacher training. They were always provided with three suits and a sum of money. The girls left at 17 and went into domestic service, nursing or teacher training, they too were provided with an outfit of clothes and some money. George Müller gave his blessing to every child on leaving his care, and gave to each a Bible.

As one orphan recalled upon leaving, *'My belongings were my Bible, my clothes and half a crown and, best of all, was the priceless blessing of George Müller's prayers.'*

Despite George Müller's death in 1898 the Homes continued to operate in the same way with the same principles. There are many fine testimonies to the Müller Homes but a former Müller child, Edith Larby, sums up what many of the 18,000 children who have been through the Homes can testify,

'The greatest thing that has ever happened to me was at the Müller Homes because there I learnt about the Lord Jesus. Through the teaching that had been put into my heart as a child, I gave that same heart to the Lord one day, and I have never regretted it.'

200,000 MILES OF TRAVEL

In 1875, at the age of 70, the remarkable George Müller decided to devote the next period of his life to a world-wide ministry of preaching and teaching. Long before George Müller came to this decision, through much prayer, God had been preparing the way for this work. In February 1870 his wife Mary died in their fortieth year of marriage. Though Mary Müller had devoted her life to supporting George in the work at the Homes, she would not have had the physical strength for the vast amount of travel which lay ahead. George Müller's health had been robust for many years despite his earlier ill health.

Their daughter, Lydia, married James Wright, George Müller's assistant, in 1871. Together they became more involved in the work of the Homes which relieved him from much of the pressure and responsibility.

In 1872 George Müller married Miss Susannah Sanger - a 'consistent' Christian - as he once described her, whom he had known for twenty five years. Susannah loved travel and made an ideal companion on the tours ahead.

From 1875 to 1892 George Müller was almost constantly engaged on missionary preaching journeys. Throughout his Christian life he always set out his aims and objectives before embarking upon God's work and this new area was no exception. George Müller wanted to share with a wider audience the truths he had discovered about God. Further, he desired to encourage Christians to become lovers of the Bible and test everything by the Word of God. Another of his aims was to break down the barriers of denominationalism and to promote, as he put it, *'brotherly love amongst Christians.'*

During his seventeen years of missionary travel he toured the United States of America three times, India twice and on three occasions toured Australia and the Colonies. In addition, George Müller preached in forty-two countries including China and Japan. By land and sea he travelled 200,000 miles, an extraordinary feat in the nineteenth century.

George Müller addressed meetings of up to 5,000 people at a time and was able to speak in English, French or German. In addition, his sermons were interpreted into as many as eighteen other languages. He estimated that during this seventeen year period he had addressed more than three million people.

George Müller still trusted God entirely for his every financial need. Often he had to pay sums of up to £240 for his long voyages yet no-one ever knew his needs. God provided for all of them.

Prayer was George Müller's answer to every problem, even when it came to influencing the forces of nature. In 1877 when the Müllers were aboard the ship 'Sardinian' bound for the United States, they ran into dense fog off the coast of Newfoundland, which severely slowed down their progress. George Müller told the Captain of his need to be in Quebec the following Saturday afternoon to which the Captain replied, *"That is impossible."* The Captain thought George Müller was mad when he suggested they should go to the chart-room and pray. When the Captain pointed out the density of the fog, George Müller replied, *'My eye is not on the density of the fog, but on the living God, who controls every circumstance of my life.'* George Müller restrained the Captain from praying because he was not a believer but after he himself had prayed, invited the Captain to open the door. The fog had lifted. This story was subsequently re-told by the Captain himself, who had since become a Christian.

It was on that same trip the Müllers were invited to the White House to meet President and Mrs Hayes. During his 200,000 miles, spanning seventeen years, George Müller met many of the world's leaders and influential politicians.

George Müller ended his travels in 1892 in his eighty eighth year. It had now become apparent to him the importance of his second wife, Susannah. She had greatly assisted in the circulation of thousands of tracts in many different languages and had spoken privately to thousands of people about the Christian gospel. Within two years of the conclusion of the tours she died and George Müller was again a widower. Another four years and George Müller himself had died. His funeral procession brought much of Bristol to a standstill. Here was a great man of faith whose influence had been so evident in his adopted city of Bristol, but also a man whose work and life had been a challenge to countless people worldwide.

FAMILY GROUP CARE

In George Müller's day the Homes developed along institutional lines, and with the care of more than two thousand children and some two hundred members of staff, there seemed to be no other way to meet the need. Indeed very few alterations were thought to be necessary until the end of the Second World War. The introduction of the Welfare State brought about many changes in this country, and among these was the method of caring for children.

As a result of the 1948 Children Act the Trustees decided, after much prayer, to sell the five large Homes at Ashley Down. They bought instead, smaller properties to house family groups of from ten to twelve children. It was felt that this would provide the children with a more natural environment in which to grow. Married couples were taken on as houseparents to care for the children and they were helped by assistants.

It took several years to complete the change-over and eventually the five Ashley Down Homes were all purchased by the local Education Authority in 1958. They are now used as a further education College.

The smaller family group homes were located in various parts of Bristol, Clevedon, and Weston-super-Mare. There was also a home in Backwell and a holiday home at Minehead. Each home had its own staff consisting of houseparents (a married couple), two assistants and some part-time domestic help. The emphasis was no longer on formal education, it was more concerned with healthy, emotional and physical development.

Then, all the children attended local state schools. Most of the children came from broken homes, many were emotionally deprived in one way or another and a few were quite seriously disturbed. In many ways this new approach had been vital to meet the needs. However, the basis of the Müller Homes remained the same and it was essential for all staff involved to have the same faith in God and obedience to His will. Although the nature of the Müller Homes changed considerably since George Müller's time, the same basic principle of God meeting every need, through the power of prayer, was still the same.

THE BEGINNING OF DAY CARE AND FAMILY SUPPORT

In the late 1970s it became apparent to the Directors and Trustees of the Homes that even family group care, as had been practised since the war, was no longer appropriate to meet the ever changing needs of society. Coupled with that, was the fact that children were no longer coming into residential care in sufficient numbers; local authorities and other childcare agencies preferring that the children be fostered with private families.

After much discussion and prayer it was felt that the way forward was in some way to meet the needs of whole families who for one reason or another were finding difficulties and pressures hard to bear.

For that reason, and with a continuing dependence on the guidance of God, a Day Care Centre was established, based at Glandore, one of the former children's homes, a large period house located in a residential area of Weston-super-Mare.

This Centre tried to create an environment where advice and practical help could be given to parents to enable them to maintain a level of family life that brought a sense of security and well being to the whole family. This very practical help once again flowed from the commitment of the staff to follow Christ's example.

Any one of three basic problems would make a child eligible for daily care at Glandore.

There was the problem of environment where inadequate housing and limited resources for recreation put a child's health at risk. Or where a child of pre-school age was unable to receive the care needed due to the ill health of a parent. The social problem where a single parent needed to follow employment for economic reasons, or the mother had become emotionally unstable and the child might have been at risk physically.

The Centre could care for up to 30 children in three separate groups, each looked after by two nursery nurses.

In addition to the Day Care Centre several Family Support Centres were opened in and around the district of Bristol.

A Family Support Centres differed from the Day Care Centre in this respect: whole families could be accommodated on a daily basis.

It was (and is today) a well known fact that family life is under attack with the divorce rate nationally affecting one in three families; more and more children and young people being brought before the Courts for antisocial behaviour, etc. It appeared that the source of the problems lay mainly in the homes of such children, and often through no direct fault of parents. The difficulties were sometimes financial, social or perhaps a result of inappropriate environment, or illness - physically or mental, etc.

It was at this point of crisis that the staff of the Müller Homes stepped in and offered support.

The Family Support Centres catered for over 200 families each week meeting the varying levels of their needs. The results confirmed that the change of direction was according to the will of God in that a number of families committed their lives to Christ as a result of the work of the Centres. Also many others were helped with marital relationships and family problems with which they were faced.

THE BEGINNING OF SCHOOLS WORK

In 1987 two Schools Workers were appointed, one on a full time basis and another on a part time basis. It was their responsibility to promote the Christian Gospel in schools in and around the City of Bristol. They endeavoured to set up Christian Union Groups and to encourage those that already existed. They also took morning Assemblies and were invited to take Religious Education lessons within the school curriculum. They were greatly encouraged at the response from the teaching staff of local schools and had the privilege of leading several pupils to the Lord as a result of their efforts. Great things were expected of this new outreach of the work of The George Müller Foundation.

THE CHILDREN'S WORK TODAY

One of the areas of concern to the Trustees has been the needs of children and families in the most needy parts of Bristol and Weston-super-Mare. Coupled with that the Trustees have sought to support local churches in such needy areas as they respond to the needs of children and families. Therefore, today in Bristol and Weston-super-Mare professional teams of staff seek to provide a range of services for children and families as well as providing support, encouragement and resources for local churches. As we become more community-minded we seek to extend our role in more and more areas. The following type and range of activities are typical:-

* providing day care for children at a Centre.
* helping to supervise a church-based parent and toddler group, nursery or creche.
* running a self-esteem group for children in a local primary school.
* helping and supporting parent's groups.
* teaching a Bible study for parents.
* running a children's bereavement group.
* organising a play-scheme.
* co-ordinating an anger management group for parents.
* monitoring self-help groups for parents.
* counselling.
* providing advocacy help for parents.
* helping in homes including cooking, family management skills, and general home visiting skills.
* taking an assembly, school club or being a teacher's assistant in community based primary schools.
* running an after school's club.
* assessing community needs.
* meeting with representatives of the statutory agencies. and so on ......

There are many different ways in which Christian love and care may be shared and a variety of different models of care are currently being explored. It is hoped that as those models are tried, models that can be replicated would be extended to needy areas other than those in which the work currently takes place. We are currently working in Weston-super-Mare, and in the Southmead and Lawrence Weston areas of Bristol. We are also exploring ways in which we might provide training for local churches in a variety of ways to enable them to be more effective in their work amongst children and families.

14

The schools work continues to grow and develop. As well as work in primary schools through the work outlined above, schools workers along with volunteer year team members seek to provide Christian teaching and discipling of many young people in Bristol Secondary schools. Schools work can be a very exacting and challenging activity. There is much need in our schools to provide support for teachers and especially in supporting and resourcing the challenge of teaching spiritual values within the curriculum. As this area develops so the work that George Müller began in pioneering provision continues to explore new and exciting areas of work. There are currently three schools workers and each year a year team seeks to support the work in education and community care. Training is given to year team members each Wednesday and the work links with a number of other projects which work with young people.

A number of other organisations are working in similar areas of care and for the last few years the work has developed relationships with some of those organisations. Usually called Associated Ministries, such relationships have been very beneficial for both the children's work and also for those other Charities.

HOMES FOR THE ELDERLY

The Müller Homes for children and the Scriptural Knowledge Institution are two separate and distinct Charities, administered from the same office at Müller House. In 1983 a third Charity was added to the work of the Müller Homes known as The Müller Homes for the Elderly.

As with the children and family care work, the Directors and Trustees had been praying for some time about helping to meet the needs of the elderly. This became a reality with the opening of the first Home, known as Tilsley House in Weston-super-Mare.

The Home is registered as an elderly persons residential care home for 24 persons. In many respects Tilsley House is ideally suited for the purpose of caring for the elderly. The rooms are well appointed and furnished, although residents are encouraged to bring items of their own furniture, if they prefer. The surrounding area is flat, with only two or three minutes walk to the promenade and beach. Directly apposite is the beautiful Clarence Park. Tilsley House is set within its own secluded garden. Shops and places of worship are within easy reach. Residents are encouraged to play an active part should they be so inclined, with opportunity to help tend the garden, get involved in craft activities and take part in acts of worship at appropriate times. Every effort is made for residents to live a secure and dignified life in their later years.

In addition, when a neighbouring property became available for purchase, having prayed about extending the work, the Trustees purchased the property and converted it into a number of flats in the form of sheltered accommodation supervised by a Warden. The house is called Tranquil House and being next door to Tilsley House, there is a clear continuity of care as residents in the sheltered accommodation have greater care needs.

The next development in elderly care will be in Bristol. A number of needs are evident in the Bristol area including the need for Christian residential care, as well as the need to provide care in the community for elderly people. The latter care may also be in conjunction with local churches. As this work develops so it will respond to the evident need of elderly people but will only develop as the Lord answers prayer as we seek Him in every stage.

CHRISTIAN LITERATURE

George Müller was a staunch believer in the power of Christian literature. With the setting up of SKI in 1834 George Müller became committed to the distribution of Bibles and tracts, not only in English but also in other languages. In that same year he founded a Bible Warehouse and Bookshop in Bristol and as the need increased it became necessary for this part of George Müller's work to be moved to separate premises.

Therefore, in 1852, the Bible and Tract Warehouse, and Bookshop, was opened in Park Street, Bristol. The work carried on from these premises for nearly ninety years until the Second World War, when the shop was destroyed by fire. The work was then transferred temporarily to other premises. These were in an area of Bristol which was away from the mainstream of city life and therefore the shop for many years occupied an unimportant role. After much prayer and waiting upon God, a new building was purchased in Park Street near the original site.

This shop was opened in 1957, under the title 'Evangelical Christian Literature'.

Subsequently two other branches were opened in Bath (in 1974), and in Weston-super-Mare (1984). Yet another example of the faithfulness of God. The shops carried a very wide range of Christian books and other literature, and every need was catered for from the general reader to the serious student. The fourth object of SKI is 'To aid in supplying the wants of Missionaries and Missionary Schools'. A proportion of the profits from the bookshops were sent to support missionaries in other countries and provided Bibles for people in countries where they are in short supply.

As a result of the increasing sophistication of the Christian bookselling market, it was decided in the early 1990's to sell the shops to other Christian booksellers; the business in Bath was sold to Scripture Union and the businesses in Bristol and Weston-super-Mare to an arm of Operation Mobilisation, "Send the Light". Since then, STL has taken over the SU bookshops and all three are part of STL trading under the name Wesley Owen Books and Music. The properties in Bristol and Weston-super-Mare remain under the ownership of the Müller Homes.

THE WORK OF THE SCRIPTURAL KNOWLEDGE INSTITUTION TODAY

The missionary work of SKI continues today with the same clear objectives put forward by George Müller and Henry Craik in 1834. Today missionaries and Christian workers are supported through the giving of many faithful people, literature is distributed and school workers encouraged in their work.

CONTINUING CONTACT WITH 'OLD BOYS AND GIRLS'

In the 1970's a Müller Fellowship was formed in Bristol by old boys and girls who felt called to meet regularly and to pray for their former 'family members' who had gone away from the Lord or who never received Him in the first place. Mr Müller regularly prayed for children long after they left the Homes and this work continues today with the same trust in the Lord that He answers each and every prayer in His own way and time. The Müller Fellowship organises an annual reunion which continues to provide a focus for old boys and girls.

THE GEORGE MÜLLER FOUNDATION

In order to provide an "umbrella" name for the three Charities which operate as separate distinct Charities, the generic name of The George Müller Foundation has now been used for some years. The Foundation holds substantial stocks of books and videos concerning the work and also a large amount of records, photographs and other items concerning the Homes. An increasing number of enquiries are being received for copies of records concerning 'Old Boys and Girls'. This has necessitated a computerization scheme (which is under way) which will enable much historical information to be readily accessible and capable of being easily copied.

There is a museum which is open from 9 am to 5 pm Monday - Friday, except Bank Holidays, when we will be very happy to welcome visitors. Although it is not essential it would be helpful to have advance notice of your visit. A Report is published each year which contains a continuing testimony of the faithfulness of God.

If you would like further information, please write to the Executive Director, The George Müller Foundation, Müller House, 7 Cotham Park, BRISTOL BS6 6DA. England. Tel: 0117 924 5001. Fax: 0117 924 4855.

In order to meet the changing needs of the time, both The Müller Homes for Children and The Müller Homes for the Elderly have now been incorporated as charitable limited liability companies.

Jesus Christ is the same yesterday, AND TODAY, and forever !
Hebrews 13 verse 8

THE MAIN EVENTS OF
GEORGE MÜLLER'S LIFE

1805 (September 27)	Born Kroppenstaedt, Prussia.
1825 (November)	Becomes a Christian following a visit to a small house meeting.
1829 (March)	Arrives in London to train with the London Society for Promoting Christianity among the Jews (now the Church Mission to the Jews)
1830 (May)	Falls ill. Believes he is dying.
1829 (Summer)	Convalescence in Teignmouth, Devon. Meets Henry Craik and becomes associated with founders of Brethren movement.
1830 (January)	Ends association with London Society for Promoting Christianity among the Jews.
1830	Becomes pastor of Ebenezer Chapel in Teignmouth.
1830 (August)	Marries Mary Groves (sister of Anthony Norris Groves) in Exeter.
1832 (May)	Müller and Henry Craik accept an invitation to become pastors of Gideon Chapel in Bristol.
1834	Establishes Scriptural Knowledge Institution for Home and Abroad.
1836 (April)	Opens first children's home in Wilson Street, Bristol, for thirty children. Subsequently opens three further homes in same street.
1849 (June)	Opens new purpose-built home in Ashley Down, Bristol, for three hundred children.
1857	Second Ashley Down home open.
1862	Third Ashley Down home open.
1866 (January)	Henry Craik dies.
1866	Dr Barnardo opens children's home in London.
1869	Fourth Ashley Down home open.
1870	Final Ashley Down home open. Now cares for two thousand children and employs over two hundred staff.
1870 (February)	Mary Müller dies.
1870s	Sends £10,000 abroad annually to nearly two hundred missionaries.
1871 (November)	Marries Susannah Sangar.
1875	Begins preaching tours. Travels two hundred thousand miles to forty-two countries.
1878 (January)	Meets President of United States and (with Susannah) is conducted around the White House.
1881	Church of England Children's Society opens first home.
1892 (May)	Last preaching tour ends.
1894 (January)	Susannah Müller dies.
1897 (June)	Preaches at Bethesda Chapel on occasion of Queen Victoria's Diamond Jubilee.
1898 (March 10)	Dies peacefully at 6.00 am aged ninety-two.

MÜLLER'S ORPHANAGE

3. No.1 House at Ashley Down was opened in June 1849, the first purpose-built Home. It was built of Pennant Stone, dressed with plain freestone, on land at Ashley Down which was bought by George Müller in 1846. In 1857 it housed over 300 children.

4. No.2 House opened in 1862 and by 1909 it accommodated 195 infant girls under 8 years, and 195 girls over 8 years.

No. 3.
Ashley Down Orphan Houses, Bristol.

5. No.3 House opened in 1862. In 1909 the house accommodated 440 girls over 8 years.

6. No.4 House opened in 1869. In 1909, the house accommodated 205 boys over 8 years, and 197 infant boys under 8 years, with 38 older girls to help the staff do the housework.

MÜLLER'S ORPHANAGE

7. No.5 House opened in 1870. In 1909 the house accommodated 201 infant girls under 8 years, and 239 girls over 8 years.

8. The Reception Room, where children were met before being sent to one of the five Homes. George Müller's library (centre left) has been preserved and can be seen at Müller House in Cotham Park.

9. In May 1832 George Müller was appointed joint pastor, with Henry Craik, of Bethesda Chapel in Great George Street. The large chapel was run down, with only a small congregation, but within a short time financial support came, many people became Christians and the church prospered.

ST. BRANDON'S, GT. GEORGE STREET, BRISTOL.
SENIOR SCHOOL.

10. In this 1930 aerial view of Bethesda Chapel, the square building can be seen adjoining Brandon Hill.

11. Boys in winter digging the ground outside No.4 Home c.1905, many small boys are watching.

12. Ashley Down Road from the corner of Station Road, looking in the direction of Gloucester Road. The wall of the No.1 Home is on the left by the horse and cart. A group of babies and staff with older Müller girls are out for a walk.

13. Babies from No.2 Home dressed for an outing, with light coloured dresses and frilly bonnets. The two babies on the right are in a double buggy.

14. The babies' dormitory at No.2 Home. The babies and small children are in their flowing night gowns ready for bed. The cots are well spread out, and a large protective fireguard can be seen behind the girl on the extreme right.

15. The nursery at No.2 Home, c.1900, the room is decorated for Christmas, with a traditional tree, and Christmas cards displayed on the mantlepiece.

16. The nursery at No.5 Home. Babies are sat around the table, the front row with their chairs turned round for the picture to be taken c.1905.

17. Small children's Christmas party at No.1 Home, Christmas being an occasion of special food. One year 150 pheasants were received from a donor in Cornwall.

18. Little children showing their delight at the decorated Christmas tree, at No.5 Home c.1910.

19. The kindergarten drawing class c.1900s. Each child is holding an object illustrated on the blackboard.

20. The kindergarten group from No.2 Home, neatly dressed with their white smocks. Could the game be "Ring a ring of roses"?

21. The boys schoolroom in No.3 Home, decorated for Christmas. George Müller devised a high standard of education, with a wide variety of subjects. Boys stayed at school until they were 14 years old.

22. Girls gathered for their photograph in the school-room c.1890s. George Müller employed a School Inspector to maintain high standards. In 1885 the percentage reached at their annual examinations, taking 6 subjects, was 91%. Girls stayed at school until they were 17 years of age. On leaving most girls went into domestic service, as well as nursing or teacher training.

MÜLLER'S ORPHANAGE

23. A dining room c.1890s. Older girls and staff waiting to serve a meal. There was a great variation of food, wholesome and regular, with meat for dinner, Mondays, Wednesdays and Fridays, and on Tuesdays and Sundays, a dish of rice and raisins was commonplace.

24. A dining room c.1900s, tables laid for tea time. The bread was known as "toke" because of the Grace said at meals "We thank thee Lord for these tokens of Thy Love."

25. The staff kitchen decorated for Christmas, with the staff and older girls, in front of the kitchen range where most of the cooking was done in that Home.

26. Another view of a staff kitchen again at Christmas time c.1902, with three senior staff and their girls. The text above the cooking range "Time whither dost thou flee. I travel on to eternity".

27. The kitchen staff sat down for their evening meal. The pillar decorated for the festive season, the most popular time of the year for children and staff, with presents, carols and special food.

28. The housegirls hall in No.5 Home, c.1907, Christmas being the time for taking photographs. The girls are relaxing with their sewing, they were taught to sew samplers and mend their own clothes.

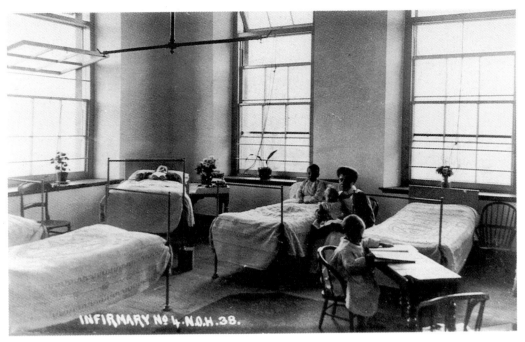

29. The Infirmary in No.4 Home, small children recovering from their illness, with their nurse. The room light and airy with many flowers and plants.

30. One of the laundry rooms c.1910. Staff with older Müller girls, ironing and folding sheets.

MÜLLER'S ORPHANAGE

31. One of the main halls where all the children gathered for special events, in this view for Christmas. On other special occasions such as George Müller's birthday each of the children were given cake and a large apple dumpling to mark the Anniversary.

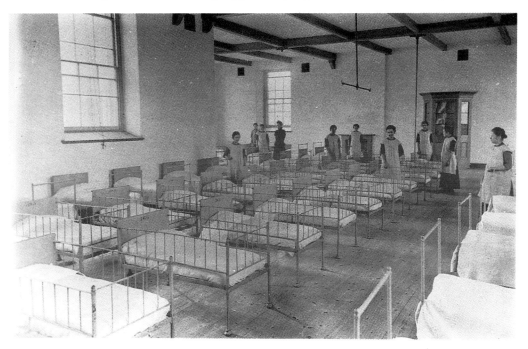

32. The babies and younger children's dormitory c.1890s. Staff and girls standing by the neatly made beds and cots, each carrying a number.

33. Older girls dressed for an outing, each carrying a picnic basket, and wearing their outdoor cloaks.

34. Another staff dining room at Christmas c.1910. Their room is beautifully decorated for the festive season.

35. Boys exercise with dumb bells c.1900s.

36. Boys from No.4 Home, enjoying a tug of war c.1910. A relaxing time for the boys, away from their busy routine.

37. A group of boys outside the swimming baths at Ashley Down before 1914.

38. The interior of the swimming baths, with diving platforms at the far end. A boy is being helped to gain confidence by swimming alongside an attendant with a ring and pole, on the right of the picture.

39. A training class at No.4 Home c.1910, boys learning the skills of woodwork, working in pairs. When the boys left school at 14 they were found a job, given a Bible, three suits, and a sum of money.

40. A woodwork class in the 1940s, teaching the boys skills for future employment. The boys never left until a job was found for them, often an apprenticeship to a trade, or farming.

41. Staff and girls working in one of the kitchens in the Homes in the early part of the century. Note the girl standing on a stool so she can reach to cut the loaf of bread.

42. Girls working in a kitchen preparing a meal, probably in the 1930s. Note the potato chipper on the table, and a steamer on the end.

MÜLLER'S ORPHANAGE

43. Station Road from the incline to Ashley Hill Station, in 1905. At least one small boy in the group to the right of the picture is a Müller boy.

44. Müller girls dressed for an outing, with their picnic baskets, maybe a trip by train to Clevedon, c.1908. They are in Station Road near the incline to the station, as in illustration 43.

45. Müller girls being counted by their teacher, as they wait to enter the station to catch their train. Each girl has a spray of flowers pinned to their shawl.

46. Ashley Hill Station, the gate can be seen where the girls in illustration 45 are standing. A group of Müller boys are sitting on the bank, a favourite pastime, watching the trains. This postcard picture c.1910.

47. Every Good Friday all the children from the five Homes, who were old enough, walked to Bethesda Chapel in Great George Street to hear George Müller preach. This annual event was still celebrated after Mr. Müller's death. The Chapel was destroyed in an air raid in the Second World War. This view taken in Ashley Down Road c.1918.

48. Boys and girls from Müller's Homes enjoying their annual outing on Purdown c.1910.

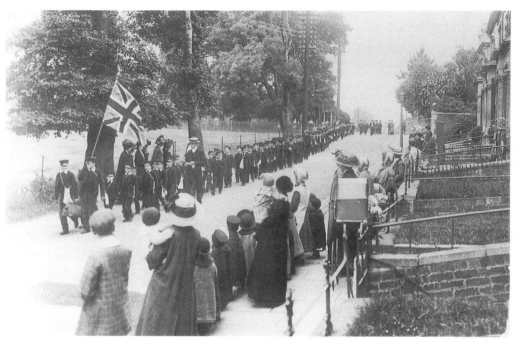

49. Two older boys carrying the Union Jack, followed by a parade of younger boys, walking down Station Road, attract attention from mothers and young children. They are on their way to watch the event to celebrate the Coronation of King George V, 1911.

50. Taken on the same day 1911, this time the younger girls marching down the road, and two small girls wearing smocks standing in the front garden of one of the terraced houses, but not taking much interest. Müller girls holding flags. Quite a crowd had gathered by the time the girls had arrived.

MÜLLER'S ORPHANAGE

51. Infants walking up Station Road, with their teachers c.1914. The fields in the distance looking towards Purdown, before Müller Road was built.

52. Toddlers with their teacher and two older girls helping to look after them, c.1914. The picture was taken outside the photographer's house, Mr. J.W. Garratt in Station Road, who also took many of the photographs in this book, and a very large number of views of Bristol.

53. The South Wales-Midland Railway line, just north of Ashley Hill station, two steam trains passing. On the skyline from left to right can be seen No.3 Home, beyond the trees No.2 Home and No.1 Home with the central tower.

54. Müller children "off for their annual outing", with picnic baskets and shawls to sit on. The line of children reaches right back to Station Road, and through the cutting under the railway line. The postcard was postally used in September 1921.

Eastville Viaduct & Park, Stapleton, Bristol. 456. E.B.P.

55. Girls from Müller's enjoying a day out in Eastville Park c.1910. The Park was purchased by Bristol Corporation in 1889. The viaduct in the distance, known as "The Thirteen Arches" connected the Clifton Down extension line with Fishponds and Staple Hill.

ST ANDREW'S PARK

56. Boys and Girls from the Homes enjoying a visit to St. Andrews Park c.1908. The land for the Park was purchased for the city in 1890, and opened in May 1895. The children are well dressed, the girls in capes and bonnets, and the boys in waistcoats, jackets, and long trousers.

MÜLLER'S ORPHANAGE

57. Müllers babies with their nurse and two older Müller girls who are helping. Yet another photograph taken outside Mr. J.W. Garratt's house in Station Road, before 1910.

58. A group of girls taken outside one of the Homes. The girls wearing white collars were known as cap girls and had special domestic duties. Date uncertain, probably about 1915.

MÜLLER'S ORPHANAGE

59. Müller girls lining Ashley Down Road, to welcome Prince Edward, Prince of Wales in June 1921, when he visited Ashley Down. No.3 Home is in the background.

60. A group of girls taken on Clevedon Pier in 1928, the children having travelled by train from Ashley Hill station.

61. Girls in their neat smocks, each holding a spray of flowers. They are all wearing their hair below their shoulders. They were allowed to do so when they were old enough to look after their own hair.

62. Phyllis Bartlett, a Müller girl who grew up in the Homes. Her routine, together with all the children, would be to rise at 6 a.m., with breakfast at 8 a.m. followed by a Bible reading and time for prayer.

63. Nursery children being cared for by two nannies on a summers day in 1938. The postcard postally used in September of that year.

64. Two groups of children having their meal outside, adjoining a play area, a swing in the background. Note the cat looking for a tit bit!

65. The nursery garden with small children playing. One of the Homes can be seen in the background, c.1930s.

66. Children out for a walk with their nanny, the children warmly dressed in the winter sunshine, each child carrying a toy.

MÜLLER'S ORPHANAGE

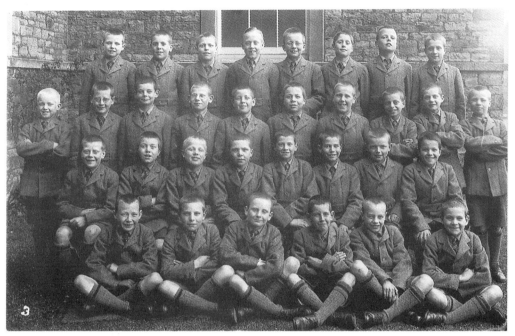

67. A group of boys taken in the early 1930s. Whilst at Müller's Homes the boys were taught to knit and darn socks, make beds, clean their shoes, scrub rooms and to work in the gardens.

68. Young girls holding their favourite toy. As they grew older the girls helped in the kitchens and sculleries, wash-houses and laundries. These girls would have been too young for these duties, but were encouraged to make their own beds and keep their rooms tidy.

69. The boys bringing their baskets full of newly dug potatoes for the two men to load into the cart and later fill the sacks lying on the ground.

70. The boys potato harvesting, with team work, which this picture shows. They are thoroughly enjoying taking part. The houses in the background are in Ashley Down Road.

MÜLLER'S ORPHANAGE

71. Boys and girls outside one of the homes, relaxing on a morning break from lessons c.1930s. Note the new uniform.

72. Girls warmly dressed ready to attend church, or visit one of the local parks c.1930s. Again, the new uniform.

73. Boys and girls join in King George V Jubilee celebrations in 1935, over the Portal of the doorway "God Save the King".

74. Another gathering for King George V Jubilee celebrations bunting trailing down, and the children listening to a Celebration address.

MÜLLER'S ORPHANAGE

75. During the 1940s children were still received and cared for, in the same way as before, as this delightful group of children shows.

76. The caption reads "Ashley Down Orphanage". Small girls playing together with their dolls and pram, a small girl with a skipping rope to the left of the picture c.1940.

77. A happy group of boys enjoying a day out, a summers day during the 1940s.

78. Another group of girls and younger children enjoy a relaxing day c.1940s.

79. A Peace and Thanksgiving Tea to celebrate the end of the Second World War. Children with flags and party hats, a happy occasion.

80. Children helping Mr. Porter and Mr. Fear unload a gift of harvest produce from the Müller Orphan Homes own van.

81. Boys gathered under the shade of a tree enjoying a day out together. Picture late 1940s, or early 1950s.

82. Another day in the summer, small children and older boys enjoying a see-saw in the nursery gardens at Müller Homes, c.1950s.

83. A 1950s view of girls enjoying a roundabout.

84. Another group of girls taken outside one of the Homes. In this 1950s picture, the girls have stopped wearing the uniform.

85. By 1958 all the children had moved from Ashley Down, and were being brought up in Family Group Homes, in Bristol, Clevedon, Weston-Super-Mare, and Minehead. All the children attended local state schools. This view shows a local firm Peglers of Bishop Road, Bishopston moving the Administration Offices to Cotham Park.

86. In 1958 the five Homes comprising of the Ashley Down Homes became the Bristol College of Science and Technology, the property of the local Education Authority. For more than one hundred years they were an orphanage, but no ordinary orphanage. It represented one man's attempt to prove to an unbelieving world that there is a God who still hears and answers prayer's. The work continues today in a different form but with the same principles of faith and prayer.